A Ride in the Night

The Story of Paul's Escape on Horseback

We are grateful to the following team of authors for their contributions to *God Loves Me*, a Bible story program for young children. This Bible story, one of a series of fifty-two, was written by Patricia L. Nederveld, managing editor for CRC Publications. Suggestions for using this book were developed by Sherry Ten Clay, training coordinator for CRC Publications and freelance author from Albuquerque, New Mexico. Yvonne Van Ee, an early childhood educator, served as project consultant and wrote *God Loves Me,* the program guide that accompanies this series of Bible storybooks.

Nederveld has served as a consultant to Title I early childhood programs in Colorado. She has extensive experience as a writer, teacher, and consultant for federally funded preschool, kindergarten, and early childhood programs in Colorado, Texas, Michigan, Florida, Missouri, and Washington, using the *High/Scope* Education Research Foundation curriculum. In addition to writing the *Bible Footprints* church curriculum for four- and five-year-olds, Nederveld edited the revised *Threes* curriculum and the first edition of preschool through second grade materials for the *LiFE* curriculum, all published by CRC Publications.

Ten Clay taught preschool for ten years in public schools in California, Missouri, and North Carolina and served as a Title IV preschool teacher consultant in Kansas City. For over twenty-five years she has served as a church preschool leader and also as a MOPS (Mothers of Preschoolers) volunteer. Ten Clay is coauthor of the preschool-kindergarten materials of the *LiFE* curriculum published by CRC Publications.

Van Ee is a professor and early childhood program advisor in the Education Department at Calvin College, Grand Rapids, Michigan. She has served as curriculum author and consultant for Christian Schools International and wrote the original *Story Hour* organization manual and curriculum materials for fours and fives.

Photo on page 5: SuperStock; photo on page 20: Peter Correz/Tony Stone Images.

Library of Congress Cataloging-in-Publication Data

Nederveld, Patricia L., 1944-
  A ride in the night: the story of Paul's escape on horseback/
Patricia L. Nederveld.
    p. cm. — (God loves me; bk. 51)
  Summary: A simple retelling of the Bible story of Paul's rescue
from his enemies. Includes follow-up activities.
    ISBN 1-56212-320-3
    1. Paul, the Apostle, Saint—Juvenile literature. 2. Bible
stories, English—N.T. Acts. [1. Paul, the Apostle, Saint.
2. Bible stories—N.T.] I. Title. II. Series: Nederveld, Patricia
L., 1944- God loves me; bk. 51.
BS2506.5.N457 1998
226.6'09505—dc21   98-15636
                                                        CIP
                                                         AC

10 9 8 7 6 5 4 3 2 1

A Ride in the Night
The Story of Paul's Escape on Horseback

PATRICIA L. NEDERVELD

ILLUSTRATIONS BY PAUL STOUB

CRC Publications
Grand Rapids, Michigan

T his is a story
from God's
book, the Bible.

It's for say name(s) of
        your child(ren).
It's for me too!

Acts 23:12-35

4

Tell everyone everywhere the good news about Jesus—that's what Paul wanted to do most. But sometimes telling people about Jesus got Paul into trouble.

Paul didn't mind—Jesus would keep him safe!

" We're glad Paul is in prison!" his enemies said to each other. "But it would be even better if we killed him. Let's try."

There was one thing Paul's enemies forgot—Jesus would keep him safe!

Someone heard their wicked plan. "Uncle Paul, Uncle Paul! Your enemies want to kill you," the boy told Paul.

But Paul remembered—Jesus would keep him safe!

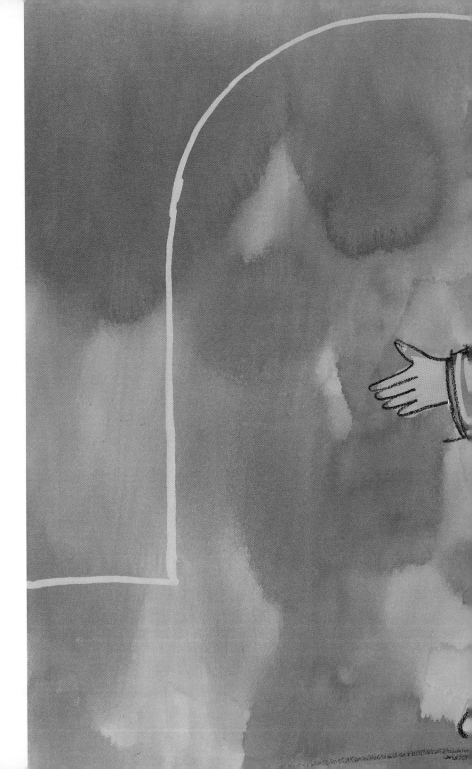

"Don't worry. Go tell the captain what you've heard," said Paul.

The little boy felt better—Jesus would keep Uncle Paul safe!

n the middle of the night, the captain sent his soldiers to rescue Paul. As Paul climbed onto his horse he remembered—Jesus was keeping him safe!

Paul galloped away into the night with soldiers all around him. Yes, Jesus *did* keep Paul safe!

wonder what Paul's enemies said when they heard about Paul's ride in the night . . .

I wonder if they knew that it was Jesus who kept Paul safe . . .

I wonder if you know that Jesus loves you and keeps you safe too . . .

Dear Jesus, thank you for loving us so much. Help us to love you like Paul did. Amen.

21

Suggestions for Follow-up

Opening

Welcome your little ones with a hug and a kind word. Express your joy that Jesus keeps them safe and brings them back together again.

Gather your little ones around you, and give each one a small blanket or soft towel. Invite them to snuggle in the blanket or towel, and talk about how blankets make us feel warm and safe. They're like a hug. God keeps us safe too. His love is like a warm blanket around us. Your little ones may enjoy holding the blanket or dragging it around with them today.

Learning Through Play

Learning through play is the best way! The following activity suggestions are meant to help you provide props and experiences that will invite the children to play their way into the Scripture story and its simple truth. Try to provide plenty of time for the children to choose their own activities and to play individually. Use group activities sparingly—little ones learn most comfortably with a minimum of structure.

1. Provide small plastic horses in your sandbox area. Draw a trail in the sand, and invite your little ones to help the horses run along the trail. If you prefer, you can draw a trail on construction paper, build one with blocks, or use Velcro or masking tape to mark a trail on the floor. Remind the children of Paul's ride in the night and how Jesus kept him safe.

2. Create an open space where children can run, jump, and hop. Older children can gallop or skip. For extra fun, create horse headbands (see Pattern X, Patterns Section, *God Loves Me* program guide) by cutting strips of paper from brown grocery bags or construction paper. Cut ears from construction paper, and glue on either side of the band; add yarn to form a mane if you wish. Pretend to be Paul's horse. Wonder about how fast the horse ran, and praise God for saving Paul.

3. Squirt a small amount of shaving cream on a table you've covered with plastic. Show your little ones how to use their fingers to walk, run, skip, and gallop through the foam. Admire the patterns they've made before you smooth out the cream and invite them to try it again. Remind your little ones that Paul knew Jesus was keeping him safe as his horse galloped along on the ride in the night.

4. Invite your children to be extra protective of the dolls and stuffed animals in your play area. Praise them for keeping their babies and pets safe. Talk about everyday times when God keeps your little ones safe.

5. Copy the hands poster (see Pattern Y, Patterns Section, *God Loves Me* program guide) on bright colored cardstock. Invite children to scribble color the hands with crayons or markers. You might want to provide small heart stickers for children to add to the poster. Help children glue a photo of themselves in the center of the cupped hands. (If you have photos of each child on file, you can make a

photocopy.) Write each child's name in the blank.

6. Sing one or more stanzas of "He's Got the Whole World" (Songs Section, *God Loves Me* program guide):

> *He's got the whole world . . .* (make large circles with arms; cup hands together)
> *He's got you and me, brother . . .* (point out, then to self)
> *He's got you and me, sister . . .* (point out, then to self)
> *He's got everybody here . . .* (join hands to form a circle)

—Words: African-American spiritual

Closing

Invite your little ones to bring their dolls and stuffed animals to your closing circle. Repeat the wondering statement on page 21, and assure each child that Jesus loves them and keeps them safe too—just like Paul. Say the prayer on page 21.

At Home

Sing "He's Got the Whole World" together at mealtime or bedtime. Help your little one think of people you can name in place of the "whole world." You might want to draw a large hand and paste snapshots of your family on the hand to remind your child that God cares for you. Throughout the week look for teachable moments to help your little one sense Jesus' loving care.

Old Testament Stories

Blue and Green and Purple Too! *The Story of God's Colorful World*

It's a Noisy Place! *The Story of the First Creatures*

Adam and Eve *The Story of the First Man and Woman*

Take Good Care of My World! *The Story of Adam and Eve in the Garden*

A Very Sad Day *The Story of Adam and Eve's Disobedience*

A Rainy, Rainy Day *The Story of Noah*

Count the Stars! *The Story of God's Promise to Abraham and Sarah*

A Girl Named Rebekah *The Story of God's Answer to Abraham*

Two Coats for Joseph *The Story of Young Joseph*

Plenty to Eat *The Story of Joseph and His Brothers*

Safe in a Basket *The Story of Baby Moses*

I'll Do It! *The Story of Moses and the Burning Bush*

Safe at Last! *The Story of Moses and the Red Sea*

What Is It? *The Story of Manna in the Desert*

A Tall Wall *The Story of Jericho*

A Baby for Hannah *The Story of an Answered Prayer*

Samuel! Samuel! *The Story of God's Call to Samuel*

Lions and Bears! *The Story of David the Shepherd Boy*

David and the Giant *The Story of David and Goliath*

A Little Jar of Oil *The Story of Elisha and the Widow*

One, Two, Three, Four, Five, Six, Seven! *The Story of Elisha and Naaman*

A Big Fish Story *The Story of Jonah*

Lions, Lions! *The Story of Daniel*

New Testament Stories

Jesus Is Born! *The Story of Christmas*

Good News! *The Story of the Shepherds*

An Amazing Star! *The Story of the Wise Men*

Waiting, Waiting, Waiting! *The Story of Simeon and Anna*

Who Is This Child? *The Story of Jesus in the Temple*

Follow Me! *The Story of Jesus and His Twelve Helpers*

The Greatest Gift *The Story of Jesus and the Woman at the Well*

A Father's Wish *The Story of Jesus and a Little Boy*

Just Believe! *The Story of Jesus and a Little Girl*

Get Up and Walk! *The Story of Jesus and a Man Who Couldn't Walk*

A Little Lunch *The Story of Jesus and a Hungry Crowd*

A Scary Storm *The Story of Jesus and a Stormy Sea*

Thank You, Jesus! *The Story of Jesus and One Thankful Man*

A Wonderful Sight! *The Story of Jesus and a Man Who Couldn't See*

A Better Thing to Do *The Story of Jesus and Mary and Martha*

A Lost Lamb *The Story of the Good Shepherd*

Come to Me! *The Story of Jesus and the Children*

Have a Great Day! *The Story of Jesus and Zacchaeus*

I Love You, Jesus! *The Story of Mary's Gift to Jesus*

Hosanna! *The Story of Palm Sunday*

The Best Day Ever! *The Story of Easter*

Goodbye—for Now *The Story of Jesus' Return to Heaven*

A Prayer for Peter *The Story of Peter in Prison*

Sad Day, Happy Day! *The Story of Peter and Dorcas*

A New Friend *The Story of Paul's Conversion*

Over the Wall *The Story of Paul's Escape in a Basket*

A Song in the Night *The Story of Paul and Silas in Prison*

A Ride in the Night *The Story of Paul's Escape on Horseback*

The Shipwreck *The Story of Paul's Rescue at Sea*

Holiday Stories

Selected stories from the New Testament to help you celebrate the Christian year

Jesus Is Born! *The Story of Christmas*

Good News! *The Story of the Shepherds*

An Amazing Star! *The Story of the Wise Men*

Hosanna! *The Story of Palm Sunday*

The Best Day Ever! *The Story of Easter*

Goodbye—for Now *The Story of Jesus' Return to Heaven*

These fifty-two books are the heart of *God Loves Me*, a Bible story program designed for young children. Individual books (or the entire set) and the accompanying program guide *God Loves Me* are available from CRC Publications (1-800-333-8300).